The Joy of Boogie and Blues

THE JOY OF BOOGIE AND BLUES is a collection of thirty-one imaginative piano solos in the early-to-intermediate grades. Some of these pieces are modern settings of standard, ever-popular folk and blues melodies, others are original compositions inspired by and built on certain styles and elements of jazz.

Essentially "blues" and "boogie," as well as "ragtime," "swing," "be-bop," are jazz styles which have emerged on the American musical scene one by one from about the turn of the century to our days. The oldest and most basic of these idioms is the blues. The prototype of the blues is a simple, but characteristic harmonic sequence of twelve measures, divided into three phrases, with a freely improvised, very expressive melody line. It probably is one of the main roots of the entire jazz idiom.

Boogie-Woogie, as developed in the twenties and thirties by Jimmy Yancey, "Pinetop" Smith, Pete Johnson and others, was originally built on the harmonic scheme of the blues. Its mood and tempo, however became quite different: more joyful and more propulsive. The essence of boogie is an ever recurring bass figure, an exuberant "basso ostinato," providing a solid background for a strongly punctuated right hand melody.

It should be noted that boogie, blues and other styles of jazz are not only domains of the popular music field, but also important and typically American contributions to contemporary music in general. The teacher and student of piano will find in this volume a colorful repertoire of most attractive solo pieces which can be integrated with the regular teaching materials with excellent results.

A few suggestions on performance: Use little or no pedal at all, especially in the faster boogie pieces; keep a steady beat throughout, but don't let your playing become stiff; let the music come through with a relaxed, natural lift and "swing."

Piano recorded by Paul Knight
Audio mixed and mastered by Jonas Persson

T0084266

To access companion recorded performances online, visit:
www.halleonard.com/mylibrary

Enter Code
2751-4332-1466-2664

ISBN 978-1-78305-023-9

HAL•LEONARD®

Visit Hal Leonard Online at
www.halleonard.com

Contact us:
Hal Leonard
7777 West Bluemound Road
Milwaukee, WI 53213
Email: info@halleonard.com

In Europe, contact:
Hal Leonard Europe Limited
42 Wigmore Street
Marylebone, London, W1U 2RN
Email: info@halleonardeurope.com

In Australia, contact:
Hal Leonard Australia Pty. Ltd.
4 Lentara Court
Cheltenham, Victoria, 3192 Australia
Email: info@halleonard.com.au

CONTENTS

Blues No. 1

Gerald Martin

Moderately slow

Boogie No. 1

2

Moderate or lively

Gerald Martin

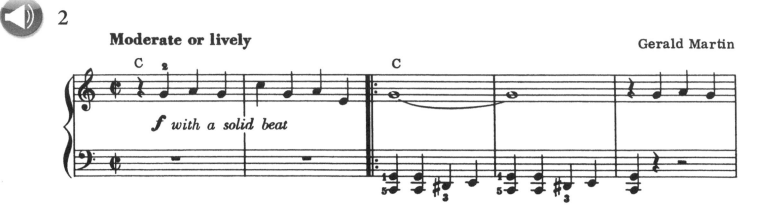

f with a solid beat

House of the Rising Sun

Folk Blues
Arr. by Gerald Martin

Old Joe Clark's Boogie

4

Gerald Martin

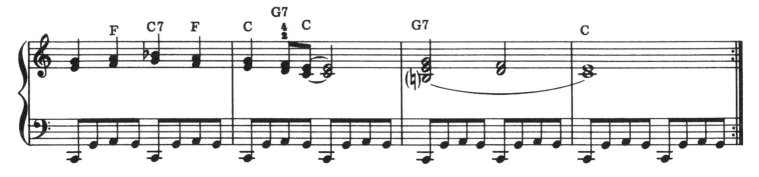

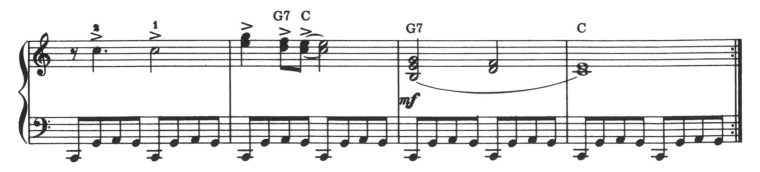

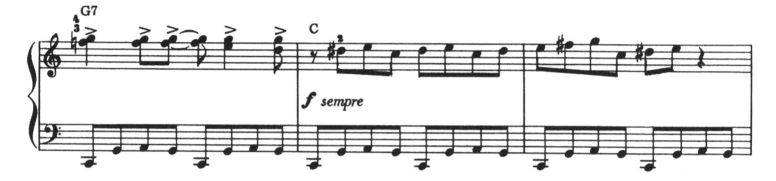

Worried Man Blues

Folk Blues
Arr. by Gerald Martin

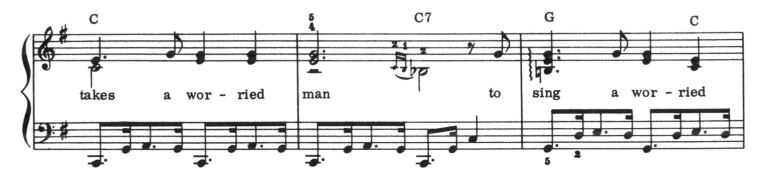

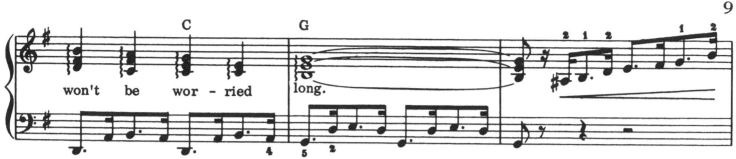

won't   be   wor – ried   long.

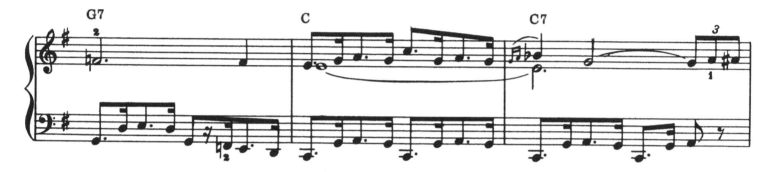

Rolling Stone

6

Moderately, with a good beat

Gerald Martin

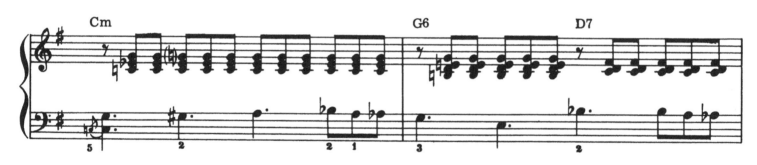

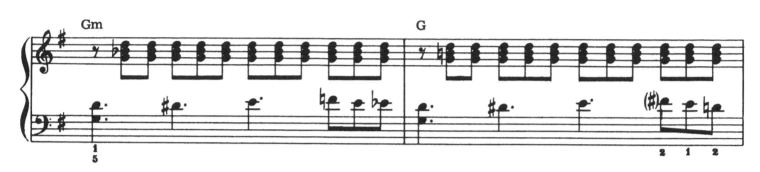

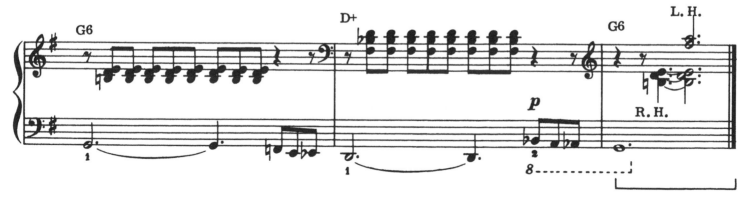

Deep Blue Sea Boogie

Gerald Martin

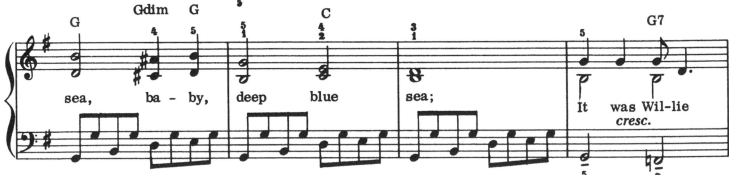

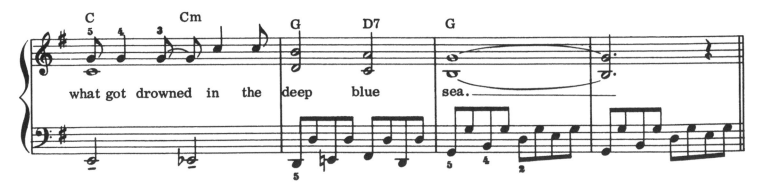

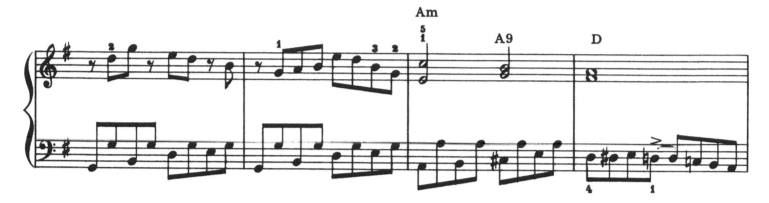

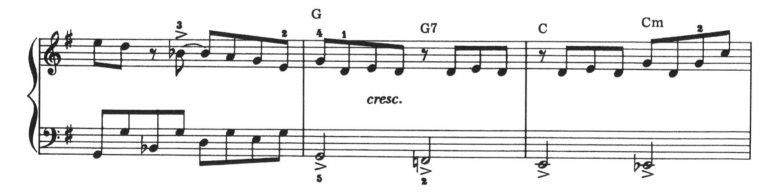

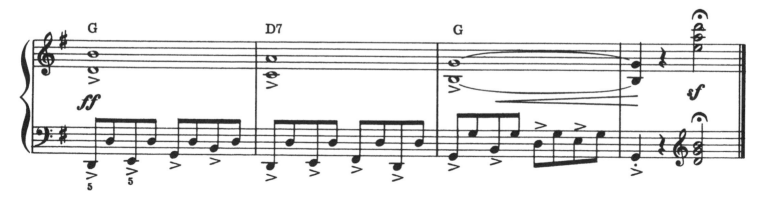

One-Track Toccata

Gerald Martin

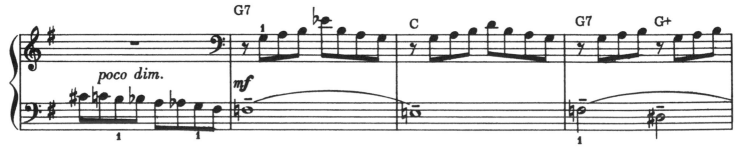

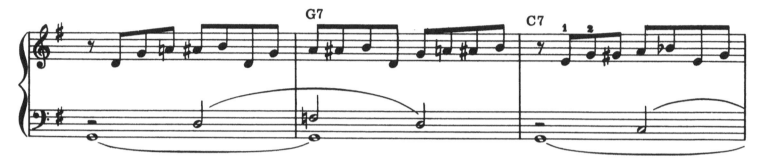

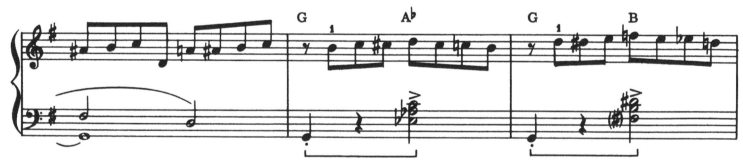

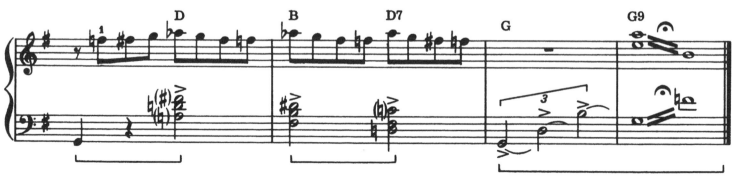

Good Night Boogie

9

Moderately, with a solid beat

Gerald Martin

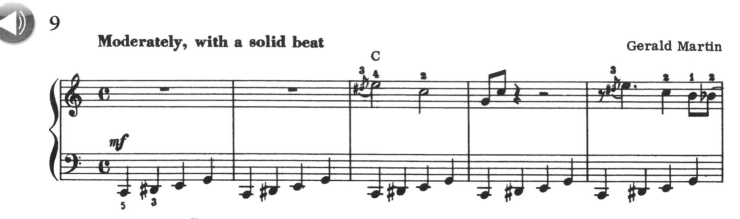

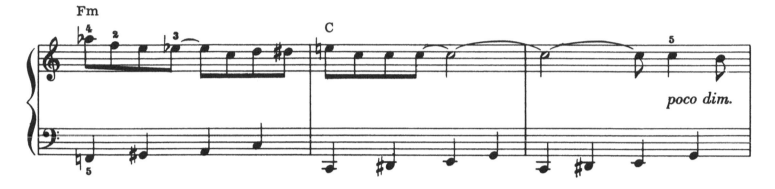

Bill Bailey Rag

Hughie Cannon —
Gerald Martin

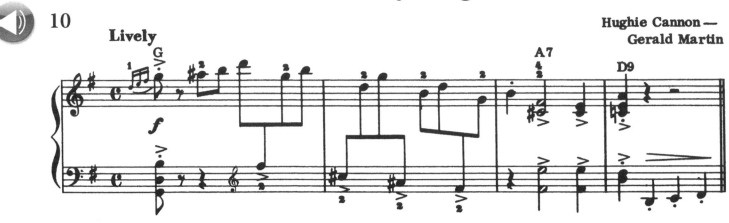

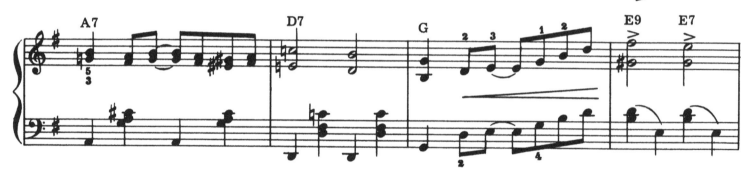

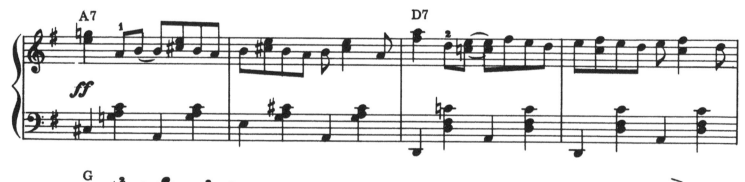

Hot and Code

11

Gerald Martin

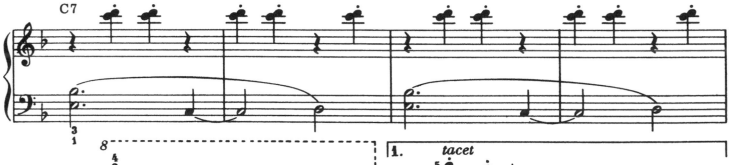

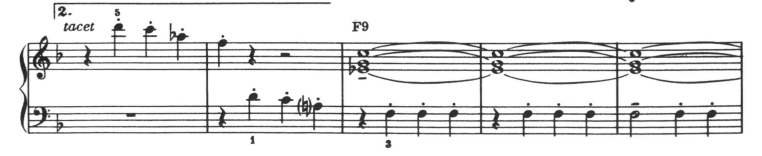

The Rock Island Line

12

Arr. by Gerald Martin

Lively "chug-along" tempo

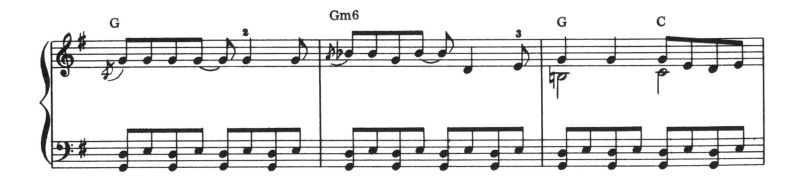

Sailors' Boogie

Gerald Martin

"The Drunken Sailor"

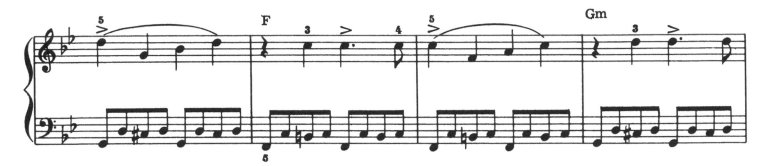

"Blow The Man Down"

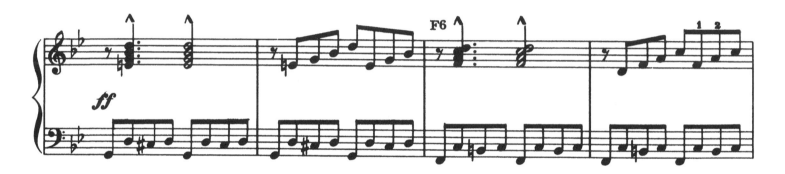

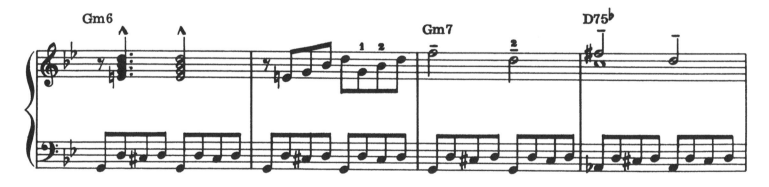

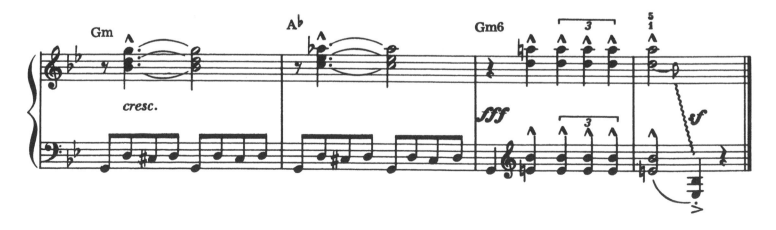

The Lonesome Road

Folk Blues
Arr. by Gerald Martin

Timber!

15

Arr. by Gerald Martin

Lively and robust

Come on pull this tim - ber 'fore the sun goes down,___ Haul it 'cross the riv-er 'fore the boss___ comes 'round___ Drag it down___ the

Moonshine Sonata

"Real Old Mountain Dew"

Gerald Martin

Comfortably rolling; with " spirit "

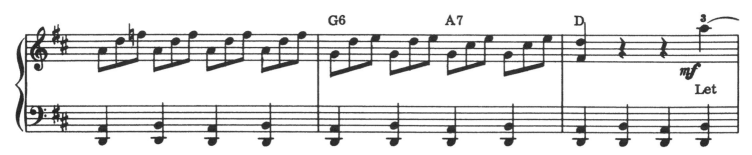

grass - es   grow and   wa - ters   flow   in   a   free   and   ea - sy

way;   But   give   me   e-nough   of   the   fine   old   stuff   that's

made   near   Gal - way   Bay.   Throw a - way   your   pills   it'll

cure all ills of pa - gan, Christ - ian, Jew, Take

off your coat and free your throat with the real old moun - tain dew.

dew.

Blues in C

17

Comfortable walking tempo

Gerald Martin

Meet Frankie and Johnny

Gerald Martin

18

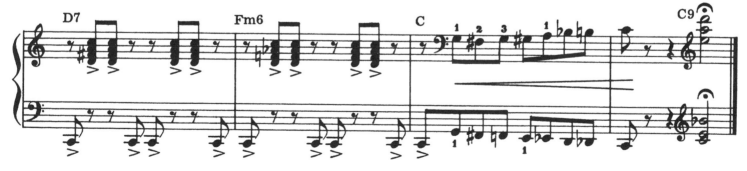

Whistling the Blues

Gerald Martin

Spiritual Boogie

Gerald Martin

20

"No Hiding Place"

There's no hid - ing

place down here; There's no hid - ing

place down here, Oh I ran to the rock to

hide my face, The rock cried out "no hid - ing place"; No hid - ing

place down here. There's

"Somebody's Knocking At Your Door"

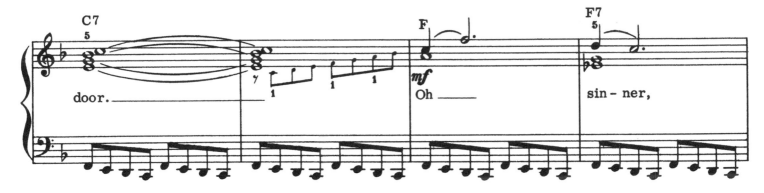

"No Hiding Place" (Variation)

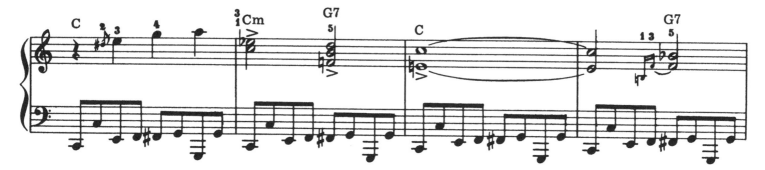

Blue Waltz

21

Denes Agay

Moderately, with a lilt

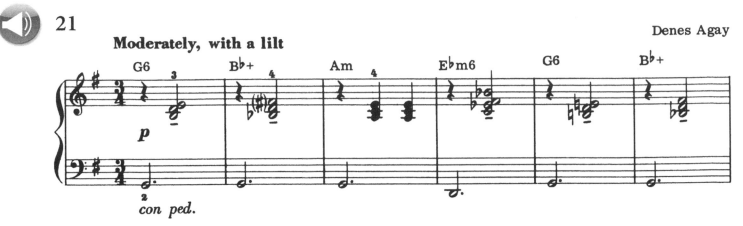

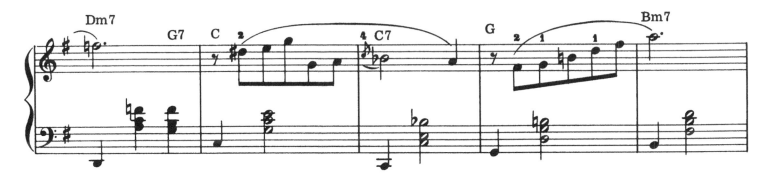

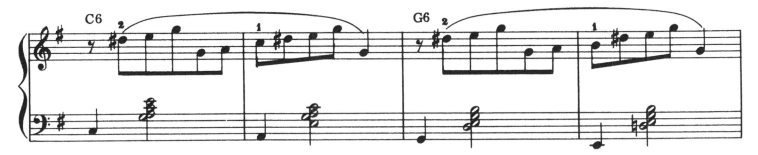

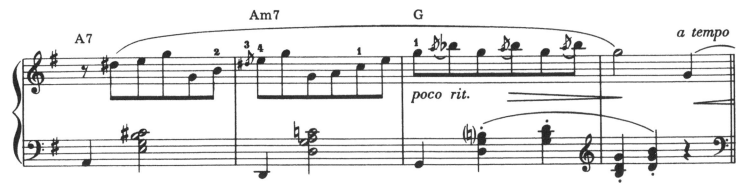

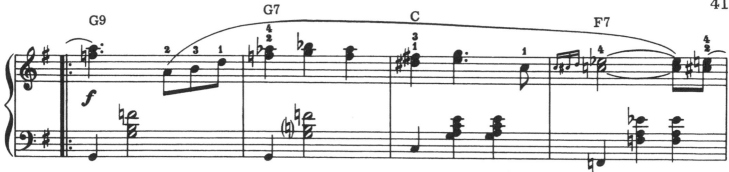

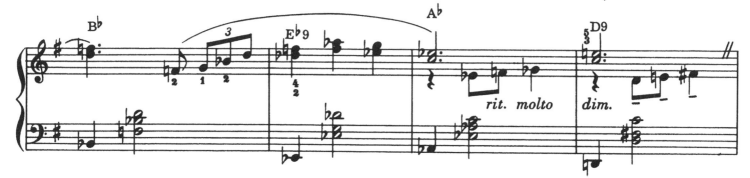

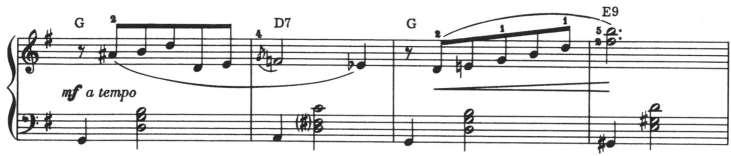

Swingin' Molly

22

Gerald Martin

Moderately, with a strong beat

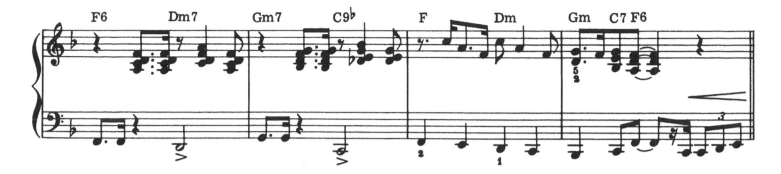

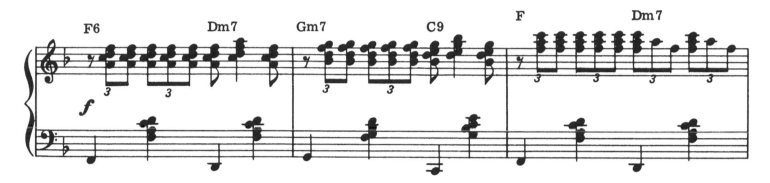

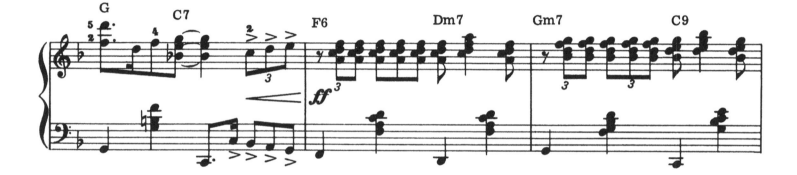

The Cotton Mill Blues

23

Moderately slow

Arr. by Gerald Martin

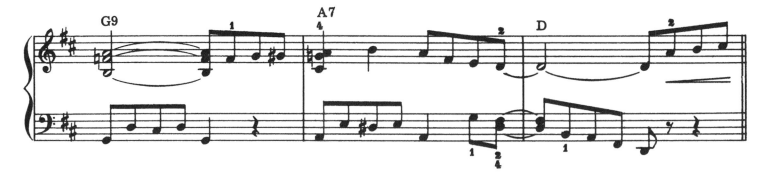

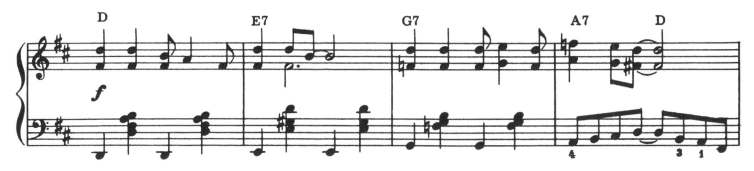

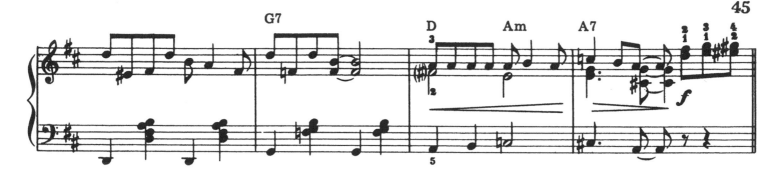

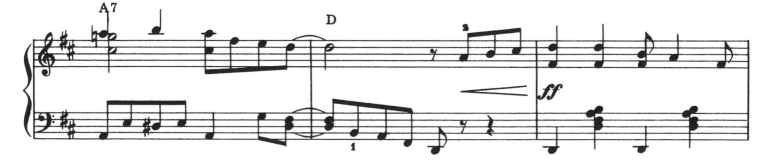

Jazz Ostinato

24

Gerald Martin

Moderately, with a solid beat

cresc. poco a poco

Safari

Denes Agay

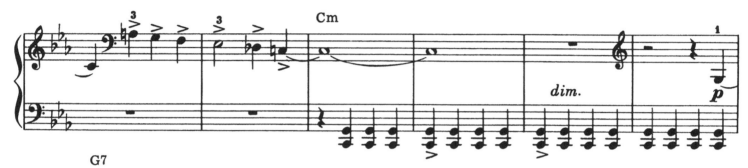

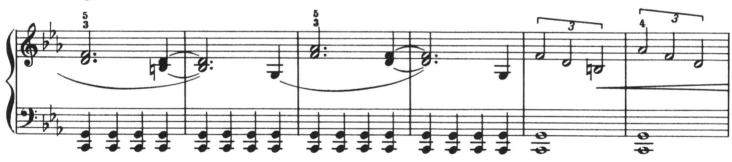

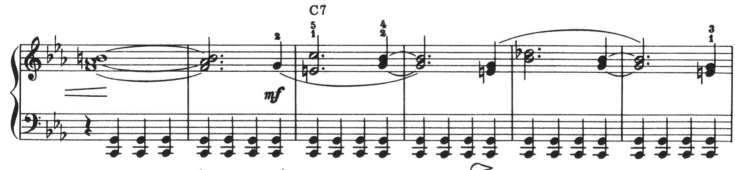

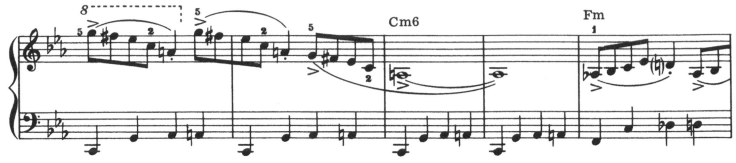

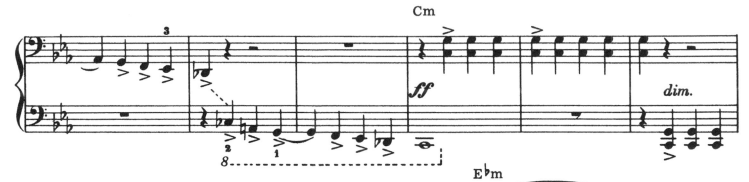

Saint James Infirmary Blues

26

Gerald Martin

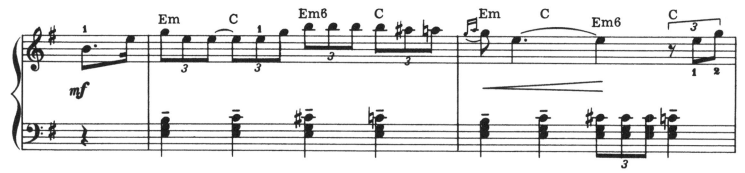

Dark-Eyes Boogie

27

Gerald Martin

Very lively

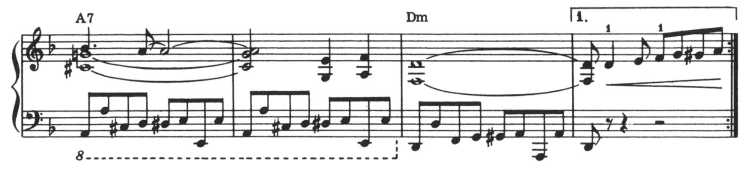

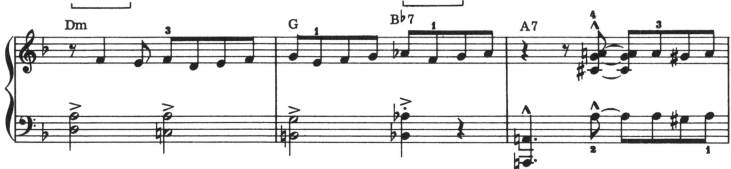

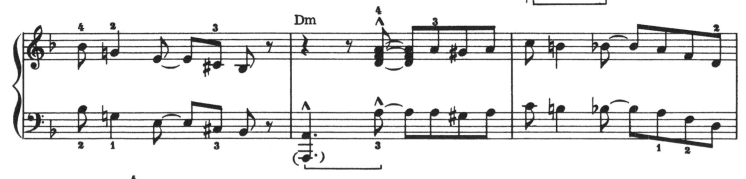

Another Shade of Blue

28

Slowly, with a free lilt

Denes Agay

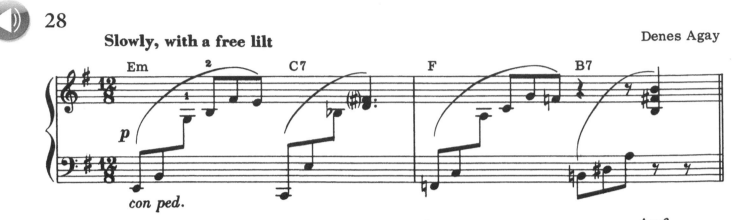

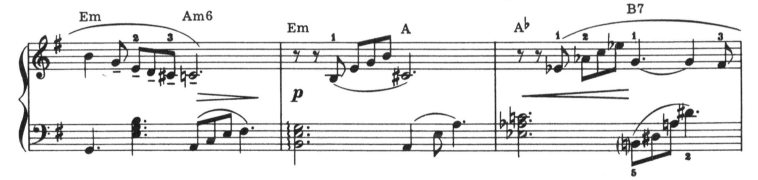

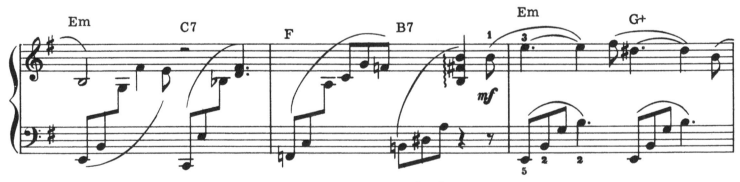

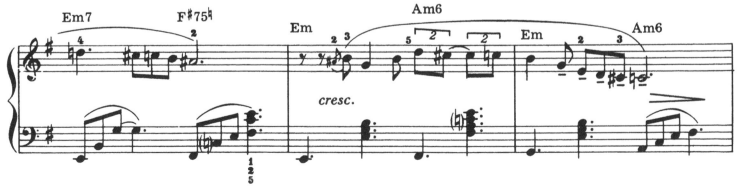

Walkin' In The Rain

29

Gerald Martin

Comfortable walking tempo

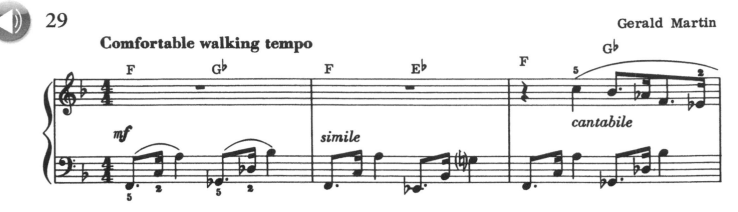

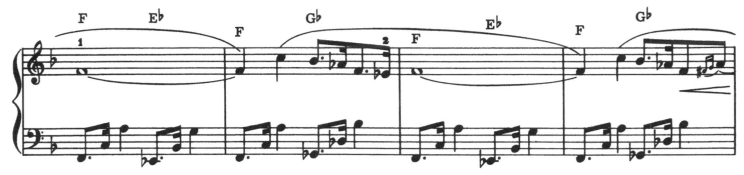

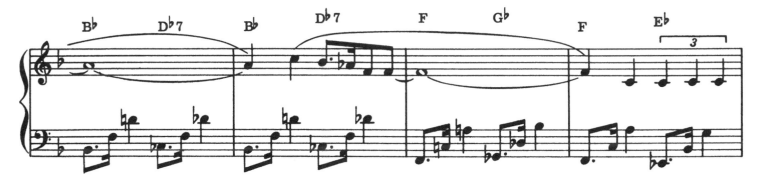

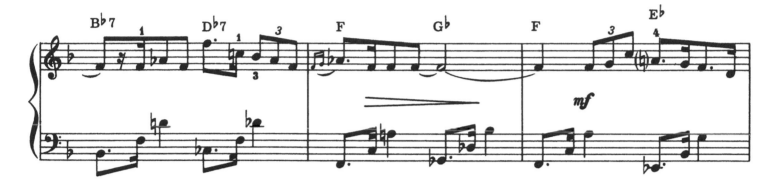

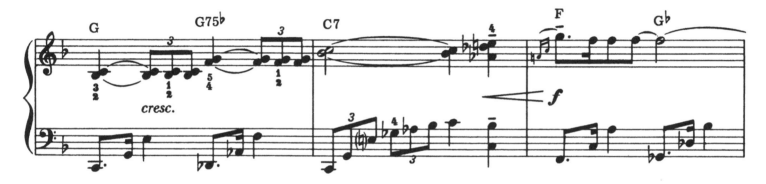

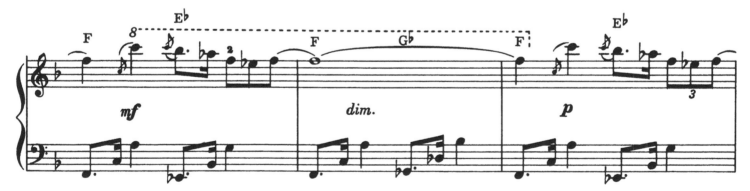

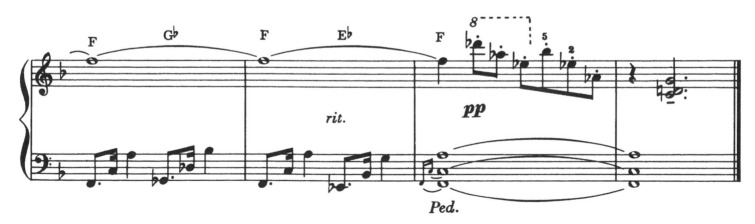

Ballad Improvisation

30

Moderately; free moving

Denes Agay

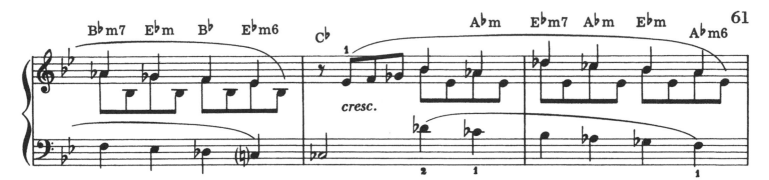

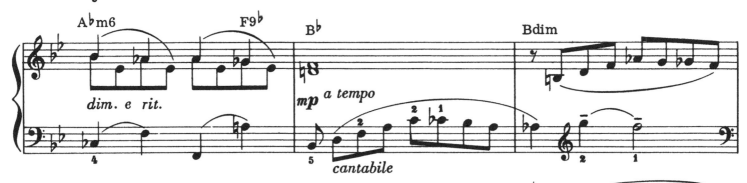

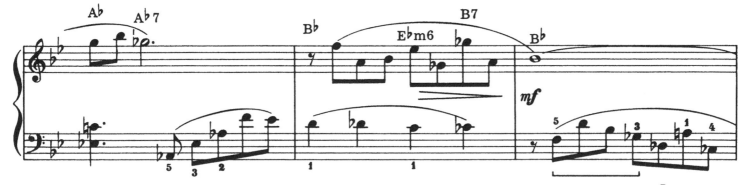

Honky - Tonky

31

As lively as possible

Gerald Martin

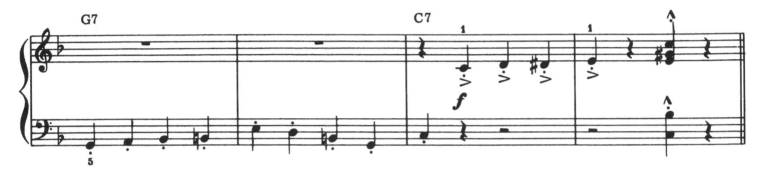

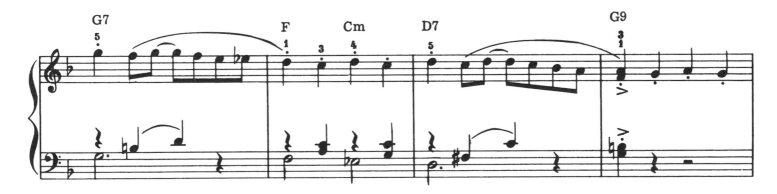

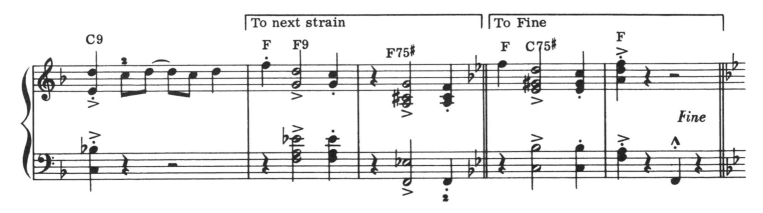

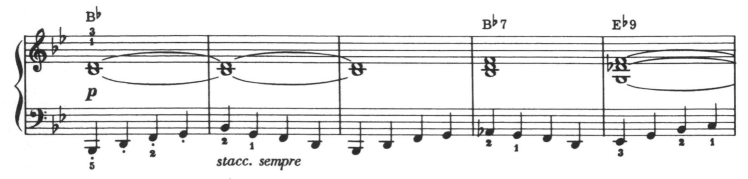

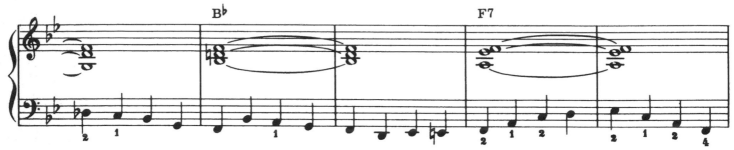

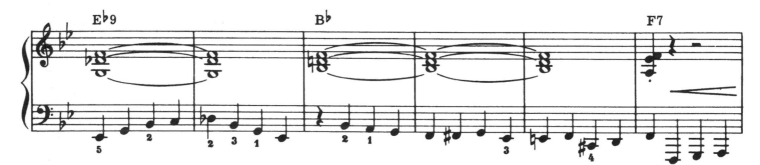

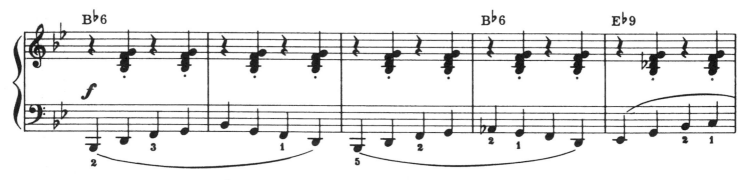

D.S. al Fine